DON YAEGER

What makes the GREAT ONES GREAT

~ *16 Characteristics of a Champion* ~

simple ▶ truths®
LEAD TO CHANGE
simpletruths.com

Editing by: Alice Patenaude

Photo Credits
Cover: front, Bread and Butter/Getty Images; back, antpkr/Thinkstock, Siarhei Makhnach/Thinkstock
Internals: page 1, Bread and Butter/Getty Images; pages 2–3, Robert Adrian Hillman/Thinkstock; pages 4–5, Irina Tischenko/Thinkstock; pages 6–7, antpkr/Thinkstock, Siarhei Makhnach/Thinkstock; page 6, Robert Adrian Hillman/Thinkstock; page 9, Fuse/Thinkstock; pages 12–13, javarman3/Thinkstock; page 23, alehnia/Thinkstock; page 28, Lane V. Erickson/Shutterstock; page 33, jordanmurph/Thinkstock; page 35, armo.rs/Thinkstock; page 36, Brocreative/Shutterstock; page 39, spxChrome/Getty Images; pages 40–41, cookelma/Thinkstock; page 50, Glen Jones/Shutterstock; page 55, Cio/Shutterstock; page 66, Comstock/Thinkstock; page 71, icsnaps/Shutterstock; page 85, Jupiterimages/Thinkstock; page 88, bikeriderlondon/Shutterstock; page 91, armo.rs/Thinkstock; page 92, Oktay Ortakcioglu/Getty Images; page 105, Alan Thornton/Getty Images; page 107, Brocreative/Shutterstock; pages 108–109, MichaelSvoboda/iStock

Published by Simple Truths, an imprint of Sourcebooks, Inc.
P.O. Box 4410, Naperville, Illinois 60567-4410
(630) 961-3900
Fax: (630) 961-2168
www.sourcebooks.com

Printed and bound in China.
LEO 10 9 8 7 6 5 4 3

CHAPTER 1

THE GREATNESS STORY

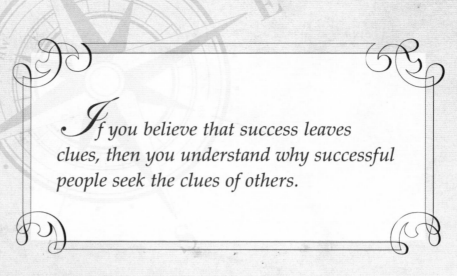

If you believe that success leaves clues, then you understand why successful people seek the clues of others.

It was May 1984. I had graduated from college and was looking forward to my first job, newspaper reporter for the *San Antonio Light*, determined to make an impact in the world.

I had stopped for a couple of days at my parents' home in Indianapolis before heading to Texas to begin my new life and career. Shortly before leaving, my father and I had a life-changing conversation.

"By choosing to be a journalist," he said, "you are going to end up in the presence of some of the most incredible people in history. You'll get that chance in sports, business, and politics. While interviewing them, make sure that there is always a moment where you learn something that is of value to *you*. Always find a moment where you ask them a question that allows you to grow."

It was profound advice that would change my life. My father was essentially telling me to find something that I could take away from the Great individuals with whom I would cross paths and then use their lessons to take myself somewhere special.

After carefully considering my father's challenge, my questions to the exceptional, high performers I interviewed became "What allowed you to do what others could not? Can you name a characteristic that gave you an advantage?"

Over the last thirty years, I have asked those questions to more than 2,500 people, including some of the Greatest winners of all time. Throughout my career as a sportswriter and author, I have not only witnessed incredible skill, but I have also had countless world-class athletes share with me the behaviors they have embraced, honed, and utilized to drive themselves to unimaginable heights. I wanted to know how they were able to do what they did for so long and how they stayed ahead of their competition year after year.

This became a long-running discussion

on what makes the Great ones Great.

Greatness is unique in that it cannot be quantified the way other statistics in sports can. Numbers are irrefutable proof of a record, such as Kareem Abdul-Jabbar's accomplishment as the highest scorer in NBA history or the undefeated record of the 1972 Miami Dolphins.

But does the achievement of those numbers make them the Greatest?

During my interviews, it appeared to me that the truly Great athletes practiced a small set of behaviors that made them dramatically better from their peers. These improvements drove their daily decisions, and the ever-so-slight differences were enough to give them an edge in their ultracompetitive professions.

Even the smallest bit of additional training or preparation can change everything. But what exactly are those small changes that can impact an individual's performance so considerably? Are they merely physical, or are they gained through intensive mental and emotional discipline? From this perspective, true Greatness is much harder to define than numbers or finishing times—because it is so much deeper than any professional ranking or record.

Taking the answers from the Greatest winners of our generation, I compiled sixteen characteristics of Greatness that can be translated into anyone's life:

1. Hating to lose more than loving to win.

2. Appreciating the value of association.

3. Placing faith in a higher power.

4. Having contagious enthusiasm.

5. Preparing for all possibilities.

6. Having no off-season.

7. **Visualizing victory.**

8. **Using adversity as fuel.**

9. **Being a responsible risk-taker.**

10. **Knowing how and when to make adjustments.**

11. **Becoming the ultimate teammate.**

12. **Being motivated by more than money.**

13. **Doing right by others.**

14. **Living with integrity.**

15. **Being a role model.**

16. **Creating a well-rounded legacy.**

*Those sixteen can be grouped
under four pillars:*

~ HOW GREAT WINNERS THINK

~ HOW GREAT WINNERS PREPARE

~ HOW GREAT WINNERS WORK

~ HOW GREAT WINNERS LIVE

A constant within these characteristics is that those who shared them were worried less about being Great than pursuing Greatness. They understood that Greatness is a journey, not a destination. It is in the chase of this principle that character develops and in that development that the routines, thoughts, and actions of Greatness begin to appear. This is a "doing" list, a series of behaviors. The quest for Greatness does not happen through wishing or through comfort and shortcuts. Greatness is both the goal and by-product of its own pursuit.

When I began this journey, I was hoping to find a secret formula that separated the talented, notable, attention-grabbing, or flashy from the athletes who seemed to have something more. What I realized is that it wasn't about a secret formula. It was about doing common things uncommonly well.

So what makes the Great ones Great?

Among those I interviewed, almost none of them gave credit to their physical gifts; there was always someone bigger, faster, and stronger than they were. Instead, the Great ones credited daily discipline and appreciation for what they had achieved—and an even Greater desire to do more. This mind-set defies human nature. Most people achieve some level of success and are satisfied with their place, but the truly Great achieve that same level of success and then ask, "What's next?"

My mentor, legendary UCLA basketball coach John Wooden, who had an incredible impact on my life, once said to me, "If you didn't have to work to get something, it probably wasn't worth getting." This is also true of Greatness: if it were easy to obtain, it wouldn't be Great—it would be commonplace.

If Great athletes, past and present, seek to consistently exhibit certain traits, then perhaps there is something in these ideas that can be applied to each of us. In this book, I am looking forward to sharing with you four of the more impactful lessons some of these Great winners provided that helped me understand what it means to be Great and how these characteristics can have a place in your life, as well.

CHAPTER 2

HOW GREAT WINNERS THINK

The pursuit of Greatness begins with having the right perspective. By studying and applying Great thinking, we can better understand the mind-set that lays the foundation for Great doing. The first pillar of Greatness is concerned with the way Great winners think, which encompasses:

- **Hating to lose more than loving to win.** They develop this mind-set by making no excuses when things don't go their way.

- **Appreciating the value of association.** They understand the importance of their inner circle.

- **Placing faith in a higher power.** They have a perspective on life, which is driven by an understanding of something bigger than themselves.

- **Having contagious enthusiasm.** Their attitudes are infectious, and they want theirs to be caught by others.

There is always a public fascination with how an athlete keeps his or her body in top physical condition, but the fascination should be on an athlete's mind, attitude, and spirit. When pursuing Greatness, consider the way you think.

*W*hat are your beliefs?

~

*H*ow do you react to the situations around you?

When I think of a takeaway moment in how Great winners think, at the top of my list would have to be a conversation I had with Coach John Wooden—the Greatest coach of all time.

Wooden was an intuitive leader and a man of immaculate character. Throughout his last twelve years as head coach at UCLA, he led the Bruins men's basketball team to an unbelievable ten national championships. He coached—and developed—some of the finest talent in college basketball, many of whom became NBA stars.

Wooden had a lifetime of advice on what makes the Great ones Great. I had an opportunity to share with him this list of the sixteen characteristics of Greatness one day, and his reaction was that outside of hating to lose—which he agreed was the first and most important characteristic of a Great winner—the second most essential characteristic he saw in Great winners was an understanding that an individual is "only as good as the team around them."

One of the most important things Coach looked for when examining a person's capacity for success was who that person included in their inner circle. "Their associations told me everything I needed to know about them," he explained. "I could tell what their future held by how important it was to surround themselves with the right people."

Coach went on to illustrate the value of association with a story about someone he described as "one of the Greatest players I ever coached." I immediately thought I was about to hear a story about Kareem Abdul-Jabbar or Bill Walton or one of the other legendary players he coached. But Wooden smiled and said, "Do you know the story of Swen Nater?" Despite being an avid basketball fan, I had not.

Swen Nater was born in the Netherlands, orphaned, and ultimately raised in Southern California. He grew to nearly seven feet tall. Although Nater had little passion for basketball, everyone encouraged him to play because of his height. However, he was so lanky and awkward that he failed to make his high school team.

A few years later, a coach from Cypress Community College approached Nater, noting that it was not easy to find seven-footers around town, and asked him if he would try basketball one more time. In exchange, the coach offered a free education, and Nater signed up. Who knows why it happens later for some people than others, but Nater—now a little older and more physically mature—grew from a kid who couldn't make his high school basketball team to one of the top five junior college centers in all of America. His game drew the attention of numerous four-year schools with premier basketball programs.

As Nater was comparing his offers, his coach at Cypress suggested they give John Wooden a call. The Bruins had just won their fifth consecutive national championship, and Nater laughed at the unlikely chance to play for the team, but he finally agreed and listened in as his coach crafted one of the Greatest sales calls of all time.

"It appears you have one scholarship left for next year, and I have your player sitting right here," the Cypress coach said to Wooden.

Wooden was baffled. He asked the coach what made him so sure. The answer surprised him. "Coach Wooden, here's your problem: As I look at your roster, you have one of the best players in the country starting at center for you next year, Bill Walton. But what you don't have is anyone big enough to compete against Bill Walton…in practice! You need *my* big guy to make *your* big guy work harder every day to get better."

The value of association immediately made sense to Wooden as he considered this pitch. What Walton needed to push him to his maximum potential was someone who could match him and challenge him every single day. Walton, Nater, the Bruins—all would be made better if these two players became a key part of the other's inner circle. After the pitch from the community college coach, Wooden was so convinced of the wisdom of this philosophy that he offered Nater the last remaining scholarship to play for UCLA.

Nater understood that taking this role would mean he would hardly see any playing time during games and certainly would not start, but his presence mattered. Nater was willing to spend his senior college career in a supporting role in order to push against the best and to surround himself with others who would build him up. Once at UCLA, he played with heart and drive and, as a result, grew daily as a player.

"I know I was brought to UCLA to make Bill Walton better," Nater once said to me. "But while pushing him, the most amazing thing happened: I got better too."

When Walton, as a senior, was primed to be the first choice overall in the NBA draft, all of the team scouts and reporters asked him the same questions: Who pushed you the hardest? Who made you work? Walton didn't mention any headline-grabbing players. Instead, he motioned down the practice court and said his Greatest challenge came from Nater.

As a result, Nater—a little-known player—became the first-ever first round NBA draft pick never to have started a senior college basketball game.

Wooden cherished this story because he understood that the value of association is an important step to achieving Greatness. He told me that Walton and Nater became Greater because they associated with each other. He told me that the Great winners are those who surround themselves with excellence, allowing others to challenge them to become better themselves. Wooden looked at me that day and offered this powerful quote: "You will never outperform your inner circle. If you want to achieve at a higher level, then always be in the improvement of your inner circle."

If you want to know what your opportunity for Greatness is, then look at the people you have around you in your personal and professional lives.

The lesson was clear, and I understood why he declared Nater as one of the Greatest players he had ever coached. Nater could have gone to another school, played more, and maybe even been a star—but he associated himself with the best he could find, and in doing so, everyone got better.

Despite never starting a college game, Nater went on to play professional basketball for twelve years before becoming an executive at Costco. To this day, Nater says that associating with Wooden and Walton was the best decision he ever made, even as Wooden and Walton still regard Nater with tremendous admiration.

Who is in your inner circle? Are they challenging and encouraging you? Do you actively seek out people and experiences that will stretch your abilities? Evaluate who can help you to be your best, to reach your full potential. Do not be content with just being good—always be driven to be, and to be around, better.

Greatness surrounds itself with Greatness. It is your duty to find those people who push you to improve, even as you return the favor to them; good-natured rivalry teaches us to work harder, celebrate others, and always keep looking ahead. We owe it to ourselves to take the opportunity to rub elbows with those who aspire to true Greatness. And if you happen to be one of those star players in your field, it is your responsibility to accept the invitation to teach others, to help them learn, and to challenge them to improve daily, just as Walton pushed Nater.

It is not how good you are when you arrive—it's what you learn from those around you that helps you grow. Accept the challenge.

Key Takeaway:
Today, look at your inner circle.
Are the people in that circle heading
in the direction you want to go?

CHAPTER 3

HOW GREAT WINNERS PREPARE

*Preparation is more than just rehearsal or practice—
it is an exact, coordinated effort that is goal-oriented and a
key driver to success. The Great ones are ready to rise to the
moment, and they never lose perspective of what they are
working toward. Greatness is not possible without deliberate
and meaningful preparation. Every Great winner I have
interviewed has stressed the importance of "being ready for
the moment." By taking daily steps toward your goal, you
are laying the foundation for your own success.*

Are you directing your time and energy to the right areas?
Are you striving for the winner's circle or just the finish
line? Great winners are always working toward their next
victory, and if they face adversity along the way, they use

it as fuel to boost themselves forward. This pillar of Greatness is built on four characteristics:

- ~ **PREPARING FOR ALL POSSIBILITIES.** THEY ARE READY BEFORE THE GAME BEGINS.

- ~ **HAVING NO OFF-SEASON.** THEY UNDERSTAND THEY ARE ALWAYS WORKING TOWARD THE NEXT GAME, AND THERE IS ALWAYS A GAME AHEAD.

- ~ **VISUALIZING VICTORY.** THEY CAN SEE WHAT SUCCESS LOOKS LIKE BEFORE THE OPENING WHISTLE.

- ~ **USING ADVERSITY AS FUEL.** THE TOUGH MOMENTS OF THEIR LIVES BECOME AN INNER FIRE.

These traits will challenge you to approach preparation in a new and more effective way.

Throughout my career in sports journalism, I can promise I have never witnessed anything close to the Greatness observed in Warrick Dunn, and few have used adversity as fuel more effectively. He is best known for his electrifying football career as a running back for Florida State University and in the NFL for the Tampa Bay Buccaneers and Atlanta Falcons, but it is his life off the field that is a true demonstration of Greatness.

Dunn was born and raised in Baton Rouge, Louisiana, and was the oldest of six children. His mother, police officer Betty Smothers, worked several part-time jobs to provide for her family.

In high school, as Dunn captured the attention of several high profile college football programs, his mother was with him, weighing the options as to which school would be the best choice for his future. After a visit from Hall of Fame coach Bobby Bowden, Dunn and his mother agreed that playing at Florida State was the right choice.

For Dunn and his family, the celebration was short-lived. A little more than two weeks after deciding on Florida State, Dunn received a call that altered the course of his life: his mother was shot and killed in an attempted bank robbery while moonlighting as a security guard.

"My mother used to tell me that adversity is promised to all of us," Dunn told me as we were writing his autobiography, *Running for My Life*. "She would say, 'In tough moments you will get two choices: you can be bitter, or you can be better. And as my child, I encourage you to choose better.'"

Dunn would never have guessed that the opportunity to make that choice—to become bitter or better in a moment of adversity—would come at eighteen years old. Devastated, overwhelmed, and confused, Dunn assumed his new role as man of the house, leader of his five younger brothers and sisters. But he did not give up on his goal to go to college to improve his future. Coach Bowden offered to let Dunn out of his verbal commitment to FSU so he could remain in Louisiana, but Dunn knew his mother would have wanted him to stay committed to Bowden. Choosing FSU was among the last decisions he had made with her, and he intended to honor the goal they had set together.

Incredibly, Dunn was able to do it all. He helped his grandmother raise his five younger siblings, all while earning a degree at FSU, becoming a national champion,

and FSU's career rushing leader. Dunn returned home every weekend he could to sort out discipline, praise, and show love to his brothers and sisters. Helping to parent his siblings at such a young age was a role he never expected, but Dunn excelled at it.

When he was chosen in the first round of the 1997 NFL draft by the Tampa Bay Buccaneers, Dunn moved his three youngest siblings to Tampa to live with him while they finished school. When his teammates would go out after practice to experience the city's nightlife, Dunn would go home to make sure the children had completed their homework and chores.

Dunn kept his family together while playing twelve impressive years in the NFL and became one of the league's all-time leading rushers. Dunn—a mere five-foot-eight and 180 pounds—was considered by many too small to have a long NFL career. He defied those odds and became only the twenty-second player in NFL history to carry the football for 10,000 yards, joining superstars Walter Payton, Emmitt Smith, and Barry Sanders on that list.

But for Dunn, the numbers off the field are the ones that matter the most. Currently, that number is well over one hundred…single parents.

Dunn established a foundation in memory of his mother that helps single parents make their dream of home ownership a reality. Each year, his Homes for the Holidays program surprises hard-working families by helping them purchase their first home. He doesn't just help them own a structure—the houses are filled with furnishings, from a fully stocked kitchen to appliances to fresh flowers and even toys for the children. Dunn personally delivers the keys. As he does so, Dunn looks the parents in the eyes and says, "Today you get to live my mother's dream."

To date, Warrick Dunn Charities has not only helped those single parents, but also their three-hundred-plus children.

"I always knew that if I ever got a shot in the NFL, I would use the opportunity to change the lives of other people," Dunn told me. "I wanted to change lives; I wanted to impact people for the long term— something that would help them on the path to better opportunities."

Because of his many philanthropic efforts, Dunn has earned the NFL's two Greatest honors for off-the-field behavior: the Walter Payton NFL Man of the Year award and the Athletes in Action/Bart Starr Award for his community accomplishments.

Dunn's life is filled with moments of Greatness; however, the story doesn't end there. While working with Dunn, I asked him what he would say if ever given the opportunity to meet the man who killed his mother. He said he had not previously given that question any thought. Dunn had spent years in counseling dealing with his grief and struggling with his own fear of loving anyone again or ever having a family of his own, because the pain of losing his mother still dominated his life.

However, Dunn finally realized that the only way to move forward was to break free. He made the decision to visit his mother's killer, going face-to-face with the man for the first time. I was fortunate to have been invited to make that trip to Angola State Prison, where he sat across the table from the other man. Dunn had brought along a spiral notebook, which was filled with the questions he wanted to ask.

Much to Dunn's dismay, however, the warden informed us when we arrived that the prisoner had recently filed an appeal with the United States Supreme Court and that Dunn may not get the closure he was looking for.

We were ushered in to meet with the prisoner, who immediately launched into a series of excuses about how his confession hadn't been legit, how he had misunderstood the questions at the trial, how he wasn't even there the night of the shooting. The confessed and convicted murderer went on and on until Dunn finally held up his hand and said, "If you didn't kill my mother, then I don't know why you are here today. But I know why I came: I'm here to forgive someone."

Both men were moved by Dunn's generous offer and tears began to flow.

As we walked out of the prison, I realized that Dunn was a living testimony to the fact that if utilized correctly, adversity fuels Greatness. The Great ones will always find an opportunity, even in the bleakest moments of their life, to use their hardship as motivation to do something special.

This dramatic challenge allowed Dunn to do just that. No one would have blamed Dunn for a lifetime of hatred; instead, he became a model of forgiveness. If his mother were alive, she'd be living in a grand house somewhere in Baton Rouge. That's what Warrick wanted for her. But because she is not—and in her memory— more than one hundred parents and three hundred children wake up each day in a house they get to call their own.

That challenge fueled Dunn to change the world.

*W*hat do you do when you come face-to-face with adversity?

Think about one or two of the most challenging times of your life and count how many positive things ultimately came from the experience. They may not have been clear immediately, but perhaps a broader perspective or a different opportunity resulted from what seemed, at the time, to be a huge setback or devastating circumstance.

Difficult times are inevitable in life, and they can bring out your best or worst behavior. Ultimately, it's up to you how you handle obstacles or setbacks. Great winners must prepare for every possibility. Dunn's mother taught him how to manage adversity, and that prepared him for that life-changing moment of forgiveness. Great winners always work toward what's ahead—and there is *always* something ahead.

Don't allow challenges to define your life. And, like Dunn, be better, not bitter.

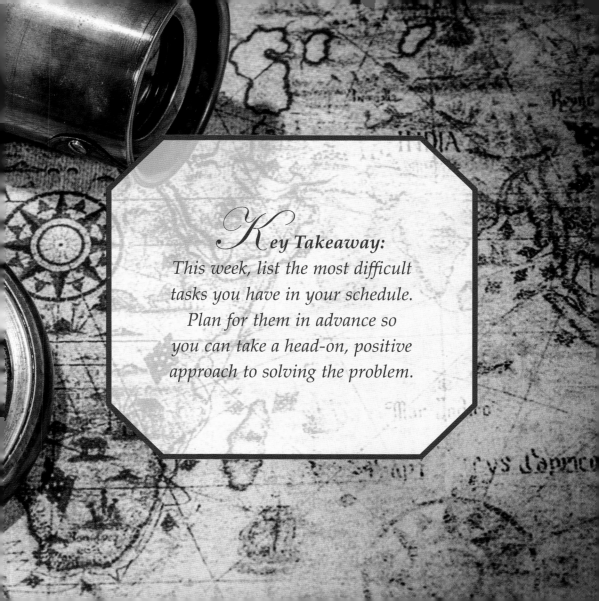

***K**ey Takeaway:*
This week, list the most difficult
tasks you have in your schedule.
Plan for them in advance so
you can take a head-on, positive
approach to solving the problem.

CHAPTER 4

HOW GREAT
WINNERS WORK

No victory worth achieving is gained without effort. How you approach your work is an important step in Greatness. What risks are you willing to take? How adaptable are you to sudden changes or strenuous circumstances? An athlete's profession is their sport, but the principles the Great ones use to dictate their approach to competition are applicable to any profession. As important as preparation is, all the practice in the world doesn't mean a thing if you don't execute on the field or in the workplace.

This pillar of Greatness encourages a closer look at how you handle your professional pursuits and involves:

~ **Being a responsible risk-taker.** The Great ones understand that most Great things occur outside of your comfort zone.

~ **Knowing how and when to make adjustments.** What got you there won't keep you there.

~ **Becoming the ultimate teammate.** They understand that even if they are the best on their team, they may have to take a different role for the team to be successful.

~ **Being motivated by more than money.** They know that if your driver is cash, you won't drive for long.

In a best-of-seven series, the hardest win to secure is the fourth one—the close-out victory. So when I think of Great winners responding to pivotal moments, Michael Jordan always seems to come to mind. I am consistently fascinated by his tenacity and extreme focus on being the best, especially in close-out moments. Today, Jordan is a living legend, but things were not always that way.

When Jordan first entered the NBA at twenty-one and at 210 pounds, he was a lousy outside shooter. In his rookie year, he made a miserable 17 percent of his three-point shots. But it didn't matter to Jordan because he was celebrated as a high-flying dunker who seemed to defy gravity. His athleticism and tremendous talent made him an overnight celebrity, and despite his poor outside shooting, he was named Rookie of the Year. However, in all of his early success, Jordan had struggled to make an impact in the NBA playoffs as his Chicago Bulls were consistently eclipsed in the Eastern Conference playoffs by their archrival, the two-time defending NBA champion Detroit Pistons.

As he grew as a leader, Jordan learned that dramatic dunks had brought fame but not necessarily victories—

especially against more dominant teams. He could score forty points a game, but that would not guarantee ultimate success in the league. To get to the next level and to stay there, longevity would require him to change his game. Jordan knew that to win a title, he would need to get more out of himself and his teammates. "Talent wins games, but teamwork and intelligence wins championships," Jordan would say later in his career.

The turning point for Jordan and the Bulls came in 1991. They were again facing the Pistons, who had knocked the Bulls out of the playoffs the previous three seasons. Over the years, the Pistons had crafted a successful strategy for defending Jordan, which included quick double-teams and very physical defense, all in an effort to throw him out of rhythm. But by the 1991 playoffs, Jordan was prepared. Through voracious practice, he added a lethal three-point shot to his arsenal and had increased his weight training to handle the physical defenses the Pistons would play.

In those 1991 playoffs, Detroit's defense was no match for Jordan's improved game. He picked apart their double-teams by passing to open teammates. When he wasn't doubled, Jordan would step back and hit longer-range shots. By adapting his game and giving his teammates what they really needed, Jordan took himself and his team to the next level. That year, the Bulls swept the Pistons in the Eastern Conference finals and Jordan won his first NBA title.

Jordan could still dunk with the best of them in the NBA, but he had to improve and change the focus of his game from dunking to shooting. By the time his career peaked, Jordan was hitting nearly 50 percent of his three-point shots, making him one of the deadliest long-range shooters in the league.

Jordan never stopped adjusting his game because he knew opponents would constantly be adjusting to him. With every changing season, he knew he would have to do something differently. Being exceptional and talented was simply the baseline, but constant adaptation was the only way to remain dominant—and successful.

What is the three-point shot for you? What is the skill you need to develop to make yourself better this year than last year? Can you recall a time when you have had to change your strategy or improve a skill to make your team successful? As professionals in the world of sports and business, we must adapt to grow. If you're not moving forward, you're moving backward. On the journey to success, embrace change and stay open-minded about making adjustments—that's what the Great ones do.

Adapting his game allowed Michael Jordan to wear six championship rings.

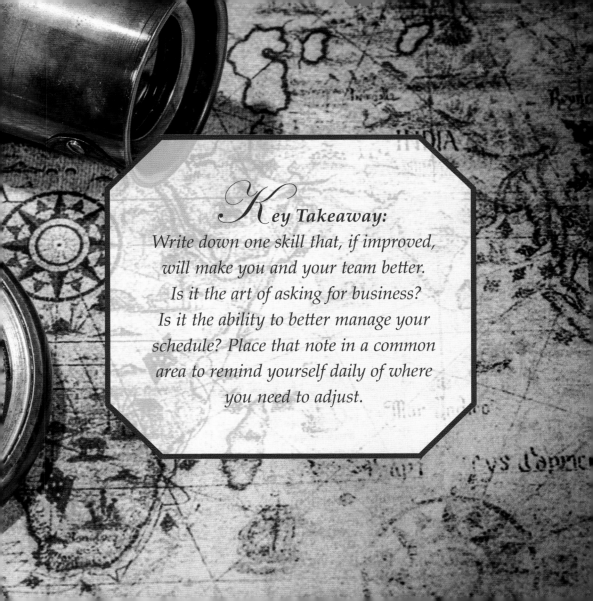

Key Takeaway:

Write down one skill that, if improved, will make you and your team better. Is it the art of asking for business? Is it the ability to better manage your schedule? Place that note in a common area to remind yourself daily of where you need to adjust.

CHAPTER 5

HOW GREAT
*W*INNERS LIVE

The fourth pillar of Greatness requires us to live our lives in a way that changes others, creating change that lasts long after we're gone. How do you show up to those around you? What do you consider your highest accomplishment? Achieving Greatness is about living a life dedicated to something bigger than yourself.

This pillar of Greatness includes:

~ **DOING RIGHT BY OTHERS.** THE GREAT ONES KNOW THAT CHARACTER IS DEFINED BY HOW THEY TREAT OTHERS, WITHOUT EXPECTING ANYTHING IN RETURN.

~ **LIVING WITH INTEGRITY.** WHEN NO ONE IS WATCHING, THEY LIVE THEIR LIVES WITH INTEGRITY.

~ **BEING A ROLE MODEL.** WHEN EVERYONE IS WATCHING, THEY SET A STANDARD FOR THOSE WHO LOOK UP TO THEM.

~ **CREATING A WELL-ROUNDED LEGACY.** THEY UNDERSTAND THEY ARE NOT DEFINED BY THEIR STATISTICS OR ACCOMPLISHMENTS.

One of the best examples of living life Greatly is Walter "Sweetness" Payton, with whom I was fortunate enough to reside while writing his autobiography.

Payton had an indomitable will while playing for the Chicago Bears, and he imposed that will on many an opponent. Throughout his illustrious career, his motto was "Never die easy." His college coach encouraged him to embrace the phrase as a running style—to gain every yard he could, to never make himself easy to tackle, and to not run out of bounds. Payton was seemingly invincible, only sitting out one game in thirteen NFL seasons, and that was because of an injury. Payton was a nine-time Pro Bowler, won a Super Bowl with the Bears in 1985, and broke Jim Brown's all-time record for career rushing yards.

Payton often noted that many fans in the stands might be able to attend only one Bears game a year and that if they saw him in that one game, he wanted them to get a snapshot of a man giving his all. Payton viewed every one of his football games as a gift, one he willingly gave to whoever might be cheering for him.

Off the field, Payton was every bit as impressive. He had a kind, loving heart and an immense desire to make a difference in people's lives. He also was very engaged with his fans; unlike many stars, he welcomed requests for autographs and seldom simply signed his name. Payton always took time to speak with the fans, a practice he said meant as much to him as it did to them.

"Too many of us only take. We don't give. Fame is what you have taken; character is what you give," Payton said to me. "I wanted to have character because football already gave me fame."

In February 1999, during an emotional press conference, Payton revealed he had a rare autoimmune liver disease and, without a liver transplant, he would die.

Later that same year, Payton contacted me about writing a book on his life. He quickly informed me that this would not be a typical autobiography but a book that would include a discussion on the great importance of organ donation.

But when I initially met with Payton, he surprised me with an update on his status. The bile-duct cancer brought on by his liver disease had spread to other organs, and now a donated liver would not save him. He had been removed from the organ donor list and had been told that he would die in a matter of months. As we sat there in his den, Payton only weighed about one hundred fifty-five pounds—a shadow of his former self—but remained jovial and upbeat, joking, "You better write fast!"

He pulled out a calendar so I could correctly share important dates from the time his illness first became apparent. The dates he circled on the calendar included his February press conference and the date he was informed that a donated liver would not save him. He then circled a date and said, "This date is big. You have to know about this day."

On that date, Payton had spent a full day filming a public service announcement to run on the popular television show *Touched by an Angel*. The PSA encouraged viewers to sign their donor cards. As I studied the dates, I could not believe what I was seeing: Payton had spent a day filming that PSA three days *after* he had been removed from the very organ donor list he was promoting. I asked him if those dates were in the correct order.

"You don't get it," he said. "We all get something in life. It's not worth a nickel if you don't give it back. Some people only take; they don't give."

Payton had decided to give by shooting that PSA, even though doing so would no longer benefit him.

On and off the field, Payton's life was about showing kindness to people in a multitude of forms. "My father told me when I was young that it was your responsibility, once you've had some success, to reach back and bring someone with you," Payton recalled.

"You cannot achieve great success without being helped along the way. Someone gave to you. That's why it is your job to give back. Do anything that might make the world a better place for someone."

Payton's advice was practical and seemingly simple. Anyone can take a moment to volunteer or to assist others in need. The beauty in this idea is that it not only nurtures the person you are helping, but also can help you learn new skills, expand your social networks, and provide an opportunity for you to explore new interests. Pay close attention to your emotions after you have freely given of yourself. Modern psychology has analyzed this euphoric feeling and termed it as "giver's high," a sensation realized after people have volunteered their time and resources for a worthy cause.

The truly Great know that character is defined by how they treat others—especially those who cannot give them anything back. By extending kindness and respect, like Payton, they make it their personal goal to touch the lives of those around them. Seemingly insignificant acts of kindness—holding a door, picking up a dropped bag, smiling at the overworked waitress—go a long way. The Great ones know that when they take the first step toward helping others, they create an important shift to someone's day and, in that small way, help to make the world a better place.

Make doing right by others a daily piece of your lifestyle. Doing so improves your path to Greatness. It is free and makes a world of difference for the individuals involved—including you, the doer. It is our responsibility to consider carefully if we are going to be people of indifference, selfishness, or vanity, or if we are going to vigorously strive toward being people of action, people of compassion—people of Greatness.

Key Takeaway:
Think of someone you know who has a current need. Challenge yourself to reach out to that individual. You could lend a helping hand, provide a resource, or just listen. Your support offers hope as he or she faces a private battle.

CHAPTER 6

CREATE YOUR
*G*REATNESS
ACTION PLAN

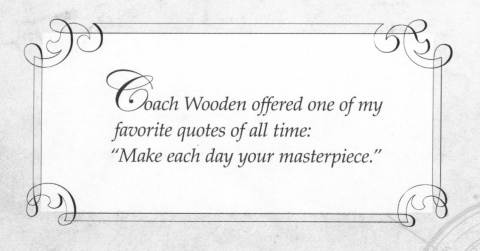

Coach Wooden offered one of my favorite quotes of all time: "Make each day your masterpiece."

This sounds simple, but it is not. If you want to make each day your masterpiece, then you'll need to plan, think, work, and live extraordinarily. Then you'll need to create your own action plan—based on the pillars of Greatness shared in this book—to improve your life daily.

After building the list of sixteen characteristics shared from these Great winners, I came up with an action plan that helps me work to achieve each one of the characteristics established. Here's my action list based on these characteristics:

*   I will make no excuses.

*   I will constantly evaluate my inner circle.

*   I will set aside time each day to recenter myself.

*   I will encourage at least one person each day.

*   I will do the necessary "homework" to make each day as productive as possible.

*   I will seek out a new opportunity for personal or professional growth each day.

*   I will envision success in all I do.

*   I will be better, not bitter, in moments of adversity.

* I will not be intimidated by taking thoughtful risks.

* I will stay open-minded.

* I will point out the contributions of others.

* I will consider what I can do to help strengthen my team.

* I will do something today for someone who cannot give me anything in return.

* I will act all day as though a person I am mentoring is sitting by my side.

* I will relish the chance to be a standard for others.

* I will remember that my life requires balance.

*S*tudy this action plan.
You'll see that there's not a single
thing here you can't do, too. If you
are consistent with this plan, then
you will see immediate impact.
You are equipping yourself to
play among the elite.

What do you need to change?

Start with a simple list of standards for yourself. Learn the lessons of Coach Wooden and the value of association by considering your inner circle. Avoid toxic friends and people, and remember to surround yourself with individuals who are headed somewhere special. Ask yourself throughout the day if you are doing just that.

Are you directing your attention toward the right places? Make preparation an integral piece of your life. Begin each morning by taking five minutes to mentally prepare for your most important tasks of the day. Evaluate both the best and the worst possible outcomes and then, if the worst does happen, learn to channel that adversity. As Warrick Dunn said, "Become better, not bitter."

What in your life can you develop that will most drive change? What is your three-point shot? Set aside time each day to pursue a new opportunity for personal or professional growth. Take a risk and introduce a new idea to your coworkers, enroll in night courses at your local college, or start writing that bestseller. Whatever you decide, do it with an open mind and a vision for your own success.

What will you do today for someone who cannot give you anything in return? Martin Luther King Jr. once said, *"Everybody can be great because everybody can serve."* Great giving is so practical because it requires little to no money. Maybe you wish to contribute more to your community, but you don't know where to start. Look around for opportunities in your daily life to show

kindness, whether it is showing respect and patience to the busy receptionist or browsing your local service organizations for volunteer opportunities.

Never be content with just being good. If you set your mind on the daily pursuit of Greatness, every one of these characteristics is achievable. Remember, Greatness is available to each of us if we are willing to do common things uncommonly well.

Go out and live your life Greatly.

"IF YOU WANT THINGS TO BE DIFFERENT, PERHAPS THE ANSWER IS TO BECOME DIFFERENT YOURSELF."

–Norman Vincent Peale, minister and author of *The Power of Positive Thinking*

Photo Credit: Gary Bogdon

ABOUT THE AUTHOR

$\mathcal{D}$on Yaeger is an eight-time *New York Times* bestselling author, acclaimed keynote speaker, and former associate editor for *Sports Illustrated*. His award-winning writing career has led to guest appearances on every major talk show in America, from *Oprah* to *Nightline* and from CNN to *Good Morning America*.

Currently living in Tallahassee, Florida, Yaeger spends much of his time sharing the lessons he's learned throughout his career with audiences across the country. He is also an entrepreneur and recognized business leader. He is currently the owner of a political consulting business and a public relations firm. Learn more at www.donyaeger.com.